A Little Bit of Me

Laura Thomas

Presentation by *BookLeaf Publishing*

Web: www.bookleafpub.com

E-mail: info@bookleafpub.com

ISBN: 9789357616638

First edition 2022

Solo

Starting solo
Sure of an inevitable path like others
Never doubting it would be.

Waiting solo
On the path awaiting a companion.
Making the best of it alone.

Continuing solo
But never alone

On The Bus

I sat on the bus and I wondered
Why my moods seemed to be so erratic?
Much like the humps in the road the bus
travelled
(Along with the rest of the traffic.)

I surmised it was hormones or such like
I always did suffer that way
Or maybe just tiredness or brain fog
At the end of a busy work day

Regardless, the need to feel better
Was prevalent sitting there on the bus
I thought about what would achieve that
With minimal effort or fuss

When suddenly the remedy struck me
Like a lightning bolt out of the blue
Something nice for tea and some chocolate
Some crisps and some haagen-daz too

Well of course it's a temporary solution
Self-medicating each day
In the long run, it causes more problems
(At least that's what the scales say)

I looked out the window and hummed
To the music playing loud in my ears
And smile to myself as the next song came on
Mad World by Tears for Fears

Music

What would we do without music?
Its very existence brings life
Every emotion is covered within
Feeling, living, alive

Cup of Tea

There's nothing quite like a nice cup of tea
To cheer you up when you feel down
Whoever thought of making a drink
Out of leaves that are murky and brown?

I would like to shake their hand
They've done the world a favour
Creating, what my Nan would call
The ultimate "Lifesaver"

Why?

Mary had a little lamb
But shouldn't we question why?
It seems a little bit odd to me
That's all, thanks then, bye

Blankety

My friend gave me a crocheted blanket
A rainbow-hued thing of delight
It really is something of beauty
And I wrap it around me quite tight

She told me that each time I'm lonely
And feel alone
to wrap it all around me,
And imagine I'm in the Lord's arms

Loneliness

Are you Lonely tonight, Elvis sang
Britney's loneliness was killing her
And Nobody wants to be Lonely
Sang Ricky Martin and Christina Aquilera

We all feel it from time to time
That hole in your soul that is gaping
And often it's difficult to fill
From your own thoughts there is no escaping

Halloween

Halloween is not for me, I'm really not a fan
I don't enjoy the ghouls and ghosts
Nor enjoy a skeleton

I find it quite offensive, to see them everywhere
And I don't understand the attraction,
to want to be willingly scared

So keep all your pumpkin obsessions
Keep your costumes and puns of the day
I'll sit this one out and resurface again when I've
got something nicer to say!

Now I know Him

Before I knew Jesus I was all in my head
I would worry and wonder and moan
I still do all those things now I know Him
But I know that I'm never alone

Faith

Faith is something personal
Something internal expressed externally

Faith isn't just there
It requires a conscious effort to have it

When we have it, we have hope.

Water

Water is calming, water is life
Water is weightlessness, floating
Water is powerful, cuts like a knife

Sing

I love to sing, it makes me whole
It makes me feel alive
I love to sing, it fills my soul
Something I can't deny

Covid

I've had covid twice since the start of it all
Luckily neither too bad
But I think of how it has impacted the world
It's all rather scary and sad

But I turn to the light and think of the good
And we keep keeping on as we do
And covid may come and covid may go
But my God is eternal and true

Happy

Hard to say.
At times I wonder if..
People can see
Perhaps they can.
Yes.

Single

When I was a child, I never imagined
That I would be single (not married)
I thought I'd be just like everyone else
Have a hubby, and children I'd carried.

But it was not to be, and I have blamed myself
Feeling shame for being "just me".
And I fight hard those feelings, I try to be strong
Advocating, so others can see...

That singleness isn't bad or wrong
Childlessness isn't a curse
I am me, I am whole, I am worthy. But sure-
-to a partner I'd not be adverse.

Hair Tail/Tale

I have a perception, that when I was little
I was generally quiet and shy
Most of the time this perception was true
But sometimes I marvel at why..
At around nine or ten, I had a hair "tail"
So 1980's, so much in the style
I just can't imagine how I pulled off the look
But I managed it all the while!
Then before I set off to secondary school
To the hair tail, I said my goodbye
I wish I had kept it, I think of those days
and I smile quite fondly and sigh

I Love Poetry (A Levelitus 1991) -written when I was 17!

A Level English Literature
Involves studying poetry
The tone, the rhythm, the structure
But those things don't matter to me

Poetry to me means feelings
Expressing them, through joining words
Who gives a damn for enjambment
(The examiners so I've heard)

So put a poem in front of me
And I'll say what I think it means
Poetry is how you interpret it
For dissecting it, I'm not to keen

But I want to pass my A Level
So I guess I'll give it a go
But that doesn't mean I'll enjoy it
I love poetry - didn't you know?

A challenge

I signed up to write, a poem each day
My intentions were good at the start
The first few were done with focus and thought
But after a while, I lost heart

I wonder if perhaps   have ADHD
Or maybe it's just me being lazy
Either way, I start things and don't follow
through
My brain gets deliberately hazy

So now it's the day before submissions are due
And I'm sat furiously writing rhyme
This isn't my best work, that is for sure
But it's what I can manage in time